Aborigines of Australia

Aborigines have lived in Australia for thousands of years. There were many different Aboriginal tribes living on their own lands until the Europeans arrived in the 1780's. They could not grow many crops on their land so the Aborigines lived a simple life gathering food and hunting. This book tells of the history and legends of the Aborigines and how they live their lives in Australia today.

PEOPLE OF THE WORLD
ABORIGINES

Anne Smith

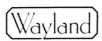

People of the World

Aborigines
Inuit
Plains Indians

All words in **bold** are explained in the
glossary on page 46.

Cover: Australian Aboriginal dancers.
Frontispiece: Happy Aborigine children jump down a sandy hillside.

This book is based on an original text by Robyn Holder.

First published in 1989 by
Wayland (Publishers) Ltd
61, Western Road, Hove
East Sussex BN3 1JD, England

© Copyright 1989 Wayland (Publishers) Ltd

Edited by Joan Walters
Designed by Ross George

British Library Cataloguing in Publication Data
Smith, Anne
  Aborigines. – (People of the world).
  1. Australian Aborigines
  I. Title II. Holder, Robyn. Aborigines of
  Australia. III. Series
  994'.0049915

  ISBN 1–85210–682–4

Typeset by: Kalligraphics Ltd, Horley, Surrey
Printed in Italy by G.Canale and C.S.p.A., Turin
Bound in France by AGM

Contents

Who are the Aborigines?

Aborigines are people who lived in Australia for many years before the British explorers came. The Aboriginal religion is called Dreaming. It tells them how to live their lives today.

An Aboriginal family took their tools and weapons with them when their **tribe** moved to a new camp.

White people came to Australia 200 years ago and made the Aborigines very unhappy. They wanted to change their way of life but the Aboriginal beliefs remained strong.
Today the Aborigines want to have the same rights as the white people of Australia. They want to decide their own future.

This is where Aboriginal tribes lived in Australia before the British explorers came.

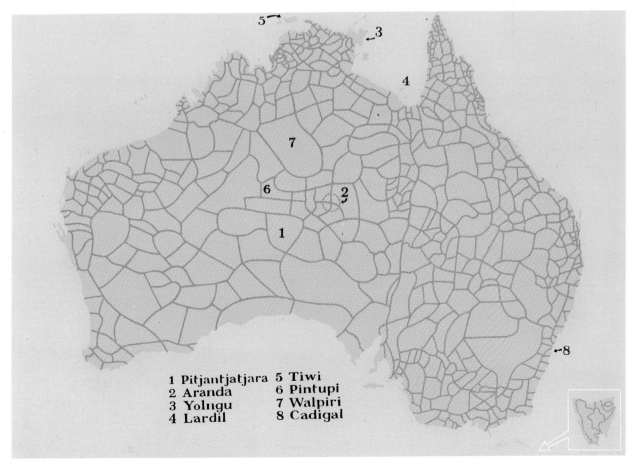

1 Pitjantjatjara   5 Tiwi
2 Aranda   6 Pintupi
3 Yolngu   7 Walpiri
4 Lardil   8 Cadigal

Chapter 1   The Dreamtime

How the world was made

Aborigines believe that the **Ancestors** lived under the ground before the world was made. They took many forms. Some were like men and women, others like plants or animals. They filled the world with light and the sun's rays warmed the earth. The Ancestors made the land, the animals, the mountains, rivers and trees.

Kundaagi, the kangaroo, is an animal Ancestor.

Then the Ancestors changed back into rocks, trees or islands. Aborigines called the time when the Ancestors lived, the Dreamtime.

Toby Naninga and Jack Nangalay own Uluru (Ayers Rock).

The **totem** of the long-necked fish-eating bird, called Niliwginei.

Aborigines have many ceremonies to link them with the Ancestors of the past and the laws of Dreamtime. By following these laws they believe they keep the past alive.

Keeping Dreamtime Laws

Aborigines believe that the spirit of the Ancestors is always with them in the land (**manta**) and the people (**anangu**). The Ancestors gave them the laws about how to live together and how to live from the land without harming it.

Aboriginal history and religion are recorded in rock paintings which are often thousands of years old.

Chapter 2   The Aboriginal people

From the land itself

Aborigines have many stories about their
Ancestors. The Aranda tribe believe they were cut
from rocks and given life by two brothers who lived
in the sky. Other tribes believe that their Ancestors
came from the sea. They all believe that they were
made by the Ancestors from the land itself, and
have lived in Australia since the world began.

This Aborigine burial ground is thousands of years
old. It has been uncovered by the wind.

An Aborigine with a
painting of the
country where he
believes his
Ancestors lived.

Aboriginal children
by a waterhole.

The many tribes

When white people first came to Australia they called all the people they found there 'Aborigines'. But the Aborigines all belonged to different tribes that spoke different languages. There were nearly 500 different Aboriginal tribes. Special ceremonies take place when tribes meet.

➡

Huts of stick and bark are made quickly when a camp is set up. Tribes living in hot dry lands made grass shelters. Tribes living in the rainy north made huts on stilts. They would move on to another place when food ran out. Sometimes they would stay in one place for six months, sometimes only for a week. Each tribe had its own special name which was also the name of its language. Tribes were made of small groups and families of children, parents and grandparents.

'My country'

Each tribe had their own particular lands which they believed had been given to them by the Ancestors – their **ngura.** They look after this special land and the Dreaming Tracks (**sacred** places) left by their Ancestors. Each tribe taught its children stories and songs about the Ancestors and the journeys they made. The songs were about hunting and tracking, and told the children about their own special territory. This Pitjantjatjara group live in central Australia.

Nagara people wait to be invited to their neighbours' camp and enter their land.

Chapter 3   Living on the land

Gathering and hunting

Aboriginal tribes did not dig, plant or harvest food. They took only the food they could gather. Women and children collected most of the family's food. They took digging sticks, **dilly bags** and wooden bowls to gather **bush tucker**. The men were hunters. They used spears and boomerangs.

Fire-stick farming helps plants to grow.

The old Dreamtime songs taught people where to get water and food from their lands. In times of plenty they would share what they had with other tribes who were hungry. Aboriginal people were happy with their way of life.

A successful fishing trip.

Honey ants (**tjala**) gathered from the bush.

The large Aboriginal family

Aborigines are kind people who care for everyone in their family and tribe. They share everything that they have. They teach their children how to behave towards the people they meet.

The different designs painted on these men show their family groups.

In an Aboriginal family all these children would be brothers and sisters.

Children feel safe and loved. They know they will be cared for by every member of their tribe. All the children of the tribe become their brothers and sisters with a special 'skin' name. They call all the adults of their family by the same name that they use for their mother or father. So everyone is a relation in one big family.

Learning

Aborigines did not have a written language or books to learn from. Children learned everything from grown-ups.

↓

While they are young the children have their own games. Boys practise spear throwing by trying to hit a rolling disc. Girls make leaf puppets and play a game called **muni-muni** to help them remember things that have happened in their family.

Children learn tribal dances and ceremonies by joining in when they are very young.

A mother teaching her children by drawing in the sand.

Becoming adults

Body-painting is
an important part
of manhood
ceremonies.

The women try to
frighten the boys
away from the men
during a ceremony.

Growing up to be an adult is important for any boy or girl. There are special ceremonies to be performed by the older people before a young girl can be called a **kunka** (young woman) or a boy can be called a man (**wati**). Boys have to learn the secrets of Dreamtime religion and law. Girls learn the ceremonies which ask for rain to fall, fruit to grow and for hunting to be successful.

Young boys sit with the older men at the start of their training for manhood.

Chapter 4   The British invasion

In 1770 Captain James Cook came to Australia. He landed on the east coast at several places to claim the country for the British King. He was supposed to ask the Aborigines to agree to this, but he asked no-one. In 1788 the British Government began sending shiploads of convicts to Australia.
The Aborigines watched the way the British behaved. They saw them lashing people with whips and chaining men together to make them work. The British took more and more land from the Aborigines. The Aborigines began to fight back.

If one white man died, ten Aborigines would be killed. In this picture the Aborigines got away.

In 1788 Governor Phillip raised the Union Jack to claim Australia for Britain.

In 1835 the British made the only **treaty** to buy Aboriginal land.

War and disease

Before the British came, the Aborigines had been healthy. If they were ever ill, they cured themselves with natural medicine. After 1788, thousands of Aborigines died from diseases like smallpox which had been brought to Australia by the British.

Captured in 1906, these Aborigine prisoners of war were chained together.

Aborigines believed that their lands had been given to them by their Ancestors and that no-one could take them away. The British did not understand this. They fought for the land.

Aboriginal warriors ready for battle.

Missionaries

Aborigines had their Dreamtime Laws, their songs
and special ceremonies. They had no need of priests.
White men and missionaries did not understand
this. They believed that Aborigines should wear
clothes and live in houses like white people. The
missionaries made the Aborigines very unhappy.
They tried to make them all live in one place and not
move around. If a child had a black mother and a
white father he was taken away from his mother
and sent to live with a white family. Others were
sent to homes to work as servants and treated badly.

These missionaries are teaching Christian hymns.

The Aborigines were told about Christianity.

The reserves

The Aborigines became poor and unhappy. They had lost their Dreaming and their lands. The government decided to make the Aborigines live together in camps called reserves. White men were put in charge of the reserves. They decided everything that the Aborigines did. When Aborigines were sent to live on a reserve, white farmers took their lands. But the reserves were not all bad. Many Aborigines felt safe there because they were living with their own people. On the big reserves they could live as they wanted to. Then the reserve became home.

This Aborigine used to live in Tasmania. Now there are no Tasmanian Aborigines.

Many Aborigines still live on their own land.

In 1946 Government
rations were tea, flour
and sugar.

Chapter 5   A people without land

Living with white people

Over the years, Aborigines had been driven from their lands by white men. Many were made to live together in reserves. During the Second World War, the army gave the Aborigines jobs as cooks, cleaners or handymen. They were paid good wages. Then the government tried to make the Aborigines live among the white men. They closed many reserves. They tried to make the Aborigines learn English and go to work every day. But this was not a success. They did not understand the Aboriginal way of life and the Aborigines would not be forced into changing it.

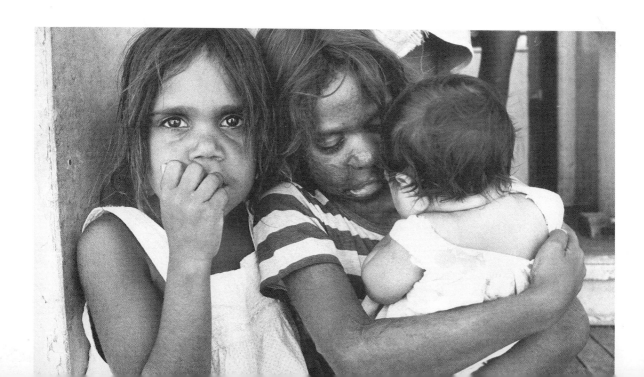

Aborigines living in
cities still perform
their special dances.

An Aborigine sells
boomerangs to tourists.

These Aboriginal
children will need
jobs when they
grow up.

Living on the edge of town

If an Aborigine had no home or job, he would have to live in a camp outside the town. The camps were crowded and dirty and there were no schools. Many children became sick and died.

Aborigines feel happy living on their own land.

Aborigines living in cities often feel confused.

Two different peoples

Australia is often called the lucky country but it
has not been lucky for the Aborigines. Nothing
that the government or the white people have
done, has helped them very much. Many white
people do not want to live close to Aborigines.
Aborigines do not want to become like white men
and women. They are two different kinds of people.

The Tent Embassy

Aborigines wanted their rights to their land returned to them. They also wanted the same rights as white Australians. In 1968 Aborigines working at Wave Hill cattle station went on strike. They wanted to be paid proper wages to work there. Eventually the government agreed to give them better pay. In 1967 Aborigines were given the right to vote and become Australian citizens. Still they did not have the same rights as white Australians. In 1972 they put up a Tent **Embassy** outside **parliament** to show the world they were still unhappy.

38

In 1975 the Australian Prime Minister returned some Gurindji land to the tribe.

In 1976 some more of their land was returned to the Aborigines, and they were allowed to claim more. Aborigines began to hope their lives were going to get better.

Chapter 6   Land rights now!

Helping themselves

Aborigines want to decide for themselves how, and where they shall live. They want the right to protect their way of life. Aborigines help their people to have better hospitals and schools. They have a legal service to help in court Aborigines.

◀ Aborigines have their own radio station.

Land Councils help them to claim back the land which has been taken from them. Since 1976 the government has agreed that the Aborigines have the right to their old tribal territories.

People are beginning to pay attention to Aboriginal beliefs and their way of life. Aboriginal art, like this beautiful bark painting is admired and respected.

Making money

Valuable minerals lie under the ground in Australia. The Aborigines do not like to have their land disturbed. But they know that they can use their land to help them have a better life.
Aborigines meet to discuss their land.

➡

SITE OF
SIGNIFICANCE

BEYOND THIS POINT LIES
AN ABORIGINAL SITE OF
A SACRED/DANGEROUS
NATURE

UNDER SECTION 69 OF THE ABORIGINAL LAND
RIGHTS (NORTHERN TERRITORY) ACT 1976

TRESPASS ON A SACRED
SITE CARRIES A PENALTY OF
$1,000
ONE THOUSAND DOLLARS.

BY REQUEST OF TRADITIONAL OWNERS

This sacred site cannot be disturbed.
Aborigines become very angry when people dig
up their land without permission. Often their
sacred places are destroyed. Many sites are
now protected by the law.

The Pitjantjatjara tell the engineers where they
can dig. They make the mining companies pay
them. If minerals are found the Pitjantjatjara take
a share of the profit. This money goes to buy trucks
or dig water wells. They also use it for radios,
hospitals and schools. In the past, mining in
Australia has ruined a lot of Aboriginal land.

'Listen to us!'

Aborigines are proud of their history. They do not want to forget their ceremonies or Dreamtime Laws. They want their children to know all about them too.

An Aboriginal family in front of the Aboriginal flag.
➡

◀ Women speaking at a tribal meeting.

In special Aboriginal schools, the children learn to
read and write in English but they also learn all
about their own special Aboriginal way of life. All
over Australia the Aborigines are working together.
Many white people are beginning to support them as
they try to gain their rights as Australians and their
rights to their lands. This map shows the land that
cannot be taken away from the Aborigines.

➡

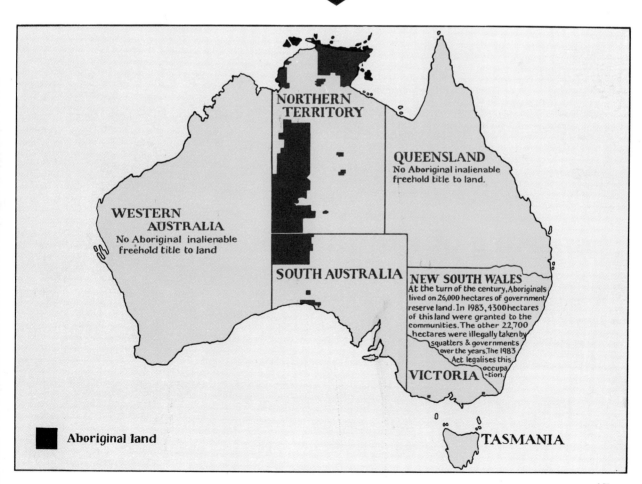

NORTHERN
TERRITORY

QUEENSLAND
No Aboriginal inalienable
freehold title to land.

WESTERN
AUSTRALIA
No Aboriginal inalienable
freehold title to land

SOUTH AUSTRALIA

NEW SOUTH WALES
At the turn of the century, Aboriginals
lived on 26,000 hectares of government
reserve land. In 1983, 4300 hectares
of this land were granted to the
communities. The other 22,700
hectares were illegally taken by
squatters & governments
over the years. The 1983
Act legalises this
occupa-
VICTORIA -tion.

■ Aboriginal land

TASMANIA

Glossary

Ancestors   The people who lived before us in our family, for example our great grandparents.

Bush tucker   Food collected in the Australian bush or outback.

Clan   A group of people who come from one of the Ancestral Beings.

Dilly bag   A small bag made of plaited grass, used for collecting food.

Embassy   The home or offices of an ambassador who represents the people of his country.

Kinship   The way in which people are related to each other.

Parliament   The place where politicians meet to discuss how a country is to be run and to make new laws.

Sacred   Highly respected and honoured especially in a religious sense.

Totem   An object, animal or plant which symbolizes a clan or family.

Treaty   An agreement between two sets of people.

Tribe   A language group. They share the same language, and one set of customs, beliefs and ceremonies.

Glossary of Pitjantjatjara words

Anangu   The people.

Kunka   A young women without children.

Manta   Land, ground or earth.

Muni-muni   A game using leaves as puppets.

Ngura   Home, camp or country. The place to which a person belongs and which belongs to that person.

Tjala   The honey ant, delicious and highly prized.

Wati   A man who has been through the ceremonies to enter manhood.

Index

Acknowledgements

The illustrations in this book were supplied by the following:

Australian Information Service, London 21, 23, (top), 27 (bottom), 39 (top), 43; Australian Institute for Aboriginal Studies 28; Bruce Coleman Ltd. (John Cancalosi) *cover*; Colorific (Penny Tweedie) 9 (bottom), 13 (bottom), 16, 18, 23 (bottom), 24 (bottom), 29 (bottom), 36 (bottom), 40; John Fairfax and Sons 36; Pamela Gill 29; Elaine Pelot Kitchener 35 (top and bottom), 40 (top); Eric Maddern *frontispiece*; Axel Poignant 8, 9 (top), 10 (top), 11, 12, 14, 17, 19 (top), 20, 25, 26, 29 (top), 30, 31 (bottom), 33 (bottom), 41 (bottom); Penny Tweedie 10 (bottom), 13 (top), 19 (top), 22, 24 (top), 34, 37, 42 (bottom). The remaining illustrations are from the Wayland Picture Library. The maps on pages 6 and 45 were supplied by Andy Martin.